THE BEST OF
CECE WINANS

ISBN 978-1-4234-3362-0

HAL•LEONARD® CORPORATION

7777 W. BLUEMOUND RD. P.O. BOX 13819 MILWAUKEE, WI 53213

Visit Hal Leonard Online at
www.halleonard.com

CONTENTS

ALABASTER BOX

Words and Music by
JANICE SJOSTRAND

With emotion

The room __ grew still __ as

last _____ she knelt be - fore His feet. And though she spoke __ no words, __ ev - 'ry - thing she said __ was heard __ as she poured her love __ for the Mas - ter from her box of al - a - bas - ter. _____ And I've come to pour __ my praise on Him like oil _____ from Mar-y's

ALL THAT I NEED

Words and Music by CECE WINANS
and KEITH THOMAS

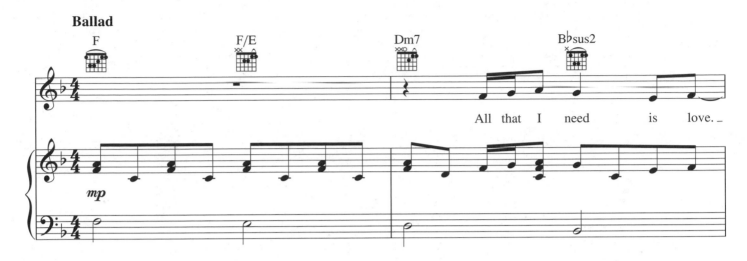

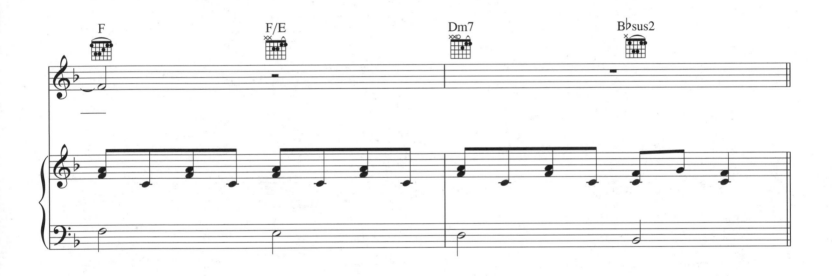

HE'S ALWAYS THERE

Words and Music by MADELINE STONE
and CECE WINANS

Lyrics (vocal line):

He's al-ways there to bright-en up your day, al-ways there in ev-'ry ___ way. ___ When it's cold and drear-y, ___ and

HALLELUJAH PRAISE

Words and Music by CECE WINANS,
CEDRIC CALDWELL and VICTOR CALDWELL

* *Recorded a half step lower.*

KING OF KINGS
(He's a Wonder)

Words and Music by CECE WINANS
and FRED HAMMOND

Energetic groove

King of kings and Lord of ___ lords, lov-er of my soul, Je - ho -

* Recorded a half step higher.

IT WASN'T EASY

Words and Music by CECE WINANS
and CHRIS HARRIS

Slow Ballad

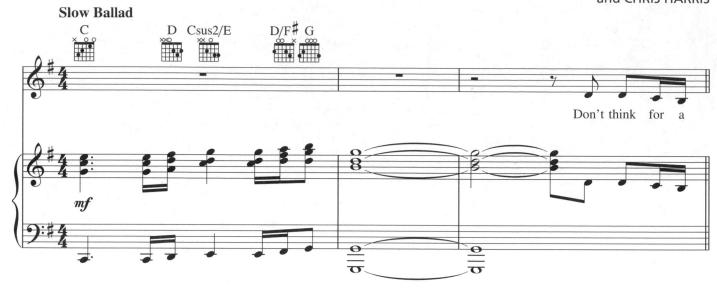

Don't think for a

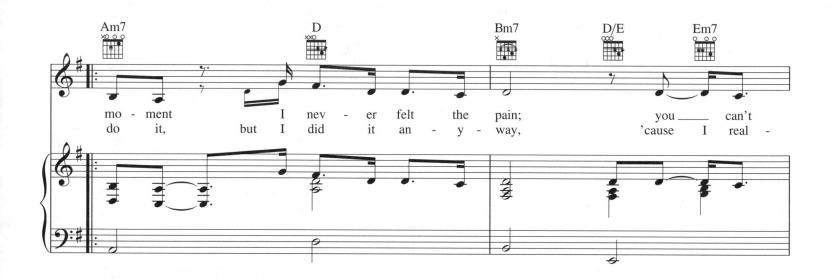

mo - ment I nev - er felt the pain; you ____ can't
do it, but I did it an - y - way, 'cause I real -

i - mag - ine ____ the hurt and ____ the shame. ____ They put the nails ____
ly love you ____ so much, I took your place. ____ I died for your sins, ____

SAY A PRAYER

Words and Music by MADELINE STONE,
CECE WINANS and DENNIS MATKOSKY

I still remember the nights when there was darkness in my life, but then You came. Something deep inside me changed, and

LOOKING BACK AT YOU

Words and Music by CECE WINANS,
WENDY WALDMAN and ADRIAN GURVITZ

Lyrics:
What can I do, _____ what wish can I make_ come true, _ be-cause you mean_ so much_ to me? _____ The love I have for

Bb/D   F7/C   Bb   Bdim7   Cm   Ab

_____ to - geth - er _____ now. _____ Just _____ look in - to _____ your _____

Fm7   A/B   N.C.

_____ heart, _____ I'll be there.   I will be the

E   B7sus/F#   A   B   Cdim7

rock for you, _ the rain _ for you, _ the sun _____ that lights _ the way _ a - cross _ the dark. _

C#m7   Amaj7   Bsus   B   G#7#5

_____ _____ No mat - ter where you are, _____ I'm nev - er ver - y

PRAY

Words and Music by CECE WINANS,
MARIO WINANS and MICHAEL JONES

I know that you

think you can't pray af-ter that mis-take, but I know it's the
gone __ too far and you've wait-ed too late, but I know that He

* *Recorded a half step higher.*

PURIFIED

Words and Music by CECE WINANS,
ALVIN LOVE III and KEITH THOMAS

Sum - mer breeze...

Life _____ is a wind -
So, _____ now I'm search -
Yeah, _____ through the liv -

Recorded a half step lower.

- ing road __ that nev - er ends, __   all _____ full of ups __
- ing for __ a he - ro, _____   some - one _____ who can help __
- ing wa - ters I __ will run, __   where _____ I will find __

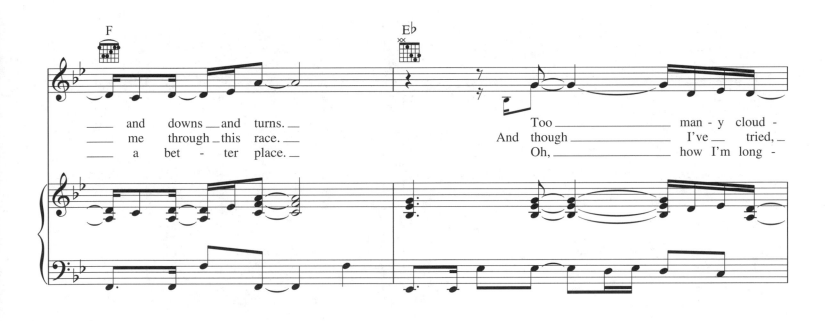

__ and downs __ and turns. __   Too _____ man - y cloud -
__ me through __ this race. __   And though _____ I've __ tried,
__ a bet - ter place. __   Oh, _____ how I'm long -

- y days __ and sleep - less nights; __ there's got - ta be __ an an - swer to __ this
__ I can't __ e - rase __ the shame; __ on - ly You __ can make __ it hap - pen. I
- ing for __ a per - fect heart; __ I need for You __ to make __ it hap - pen.

pain _____ in - side. _ | pray that You _ will make _ it hap - pen.
On - ly You _ can make _ it hap - pen.

Pu - ri - fied, _____ I wan - na be ___ pu - ri - fied. _____ I wan - na be ___

fresh like a rush - ing wa - ter in the pres - ence of the Fa - ther. ___

SLIPPIN'

Words and Music by CECE WINANS,
SYLVIA BENNETT SMITH and DECONZO SMITH

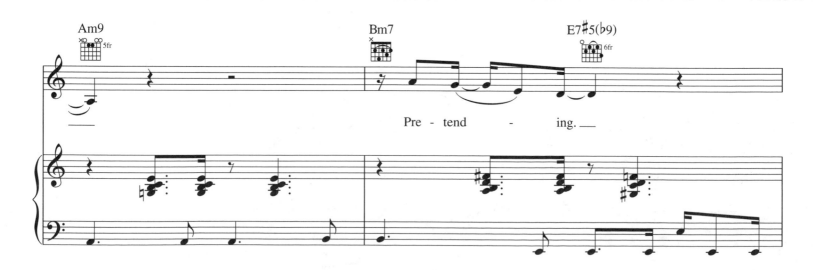

- na stay __ with me, ___ I need hon __ - __ es - ty. ___ Don't play with me, you're slip-

- pin'. _____ Can't __ make it on __ your own; __ - es - ty. ___ Don't play with me, you're slip -
Pre -

- pin'. _____
tend-ing ev-'ry-thing is o - kay in front of the crowd, _____ you're smil - in'. ___ But

THRONE ROOM

Words and Music by CECE WINANS
and ANDRAÉ CROUCH

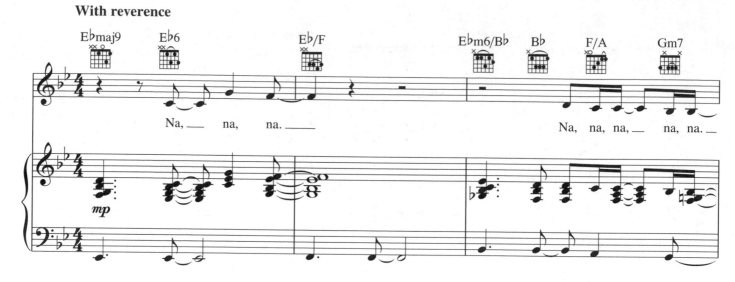

Wel - come   to   the   Throne   Room.

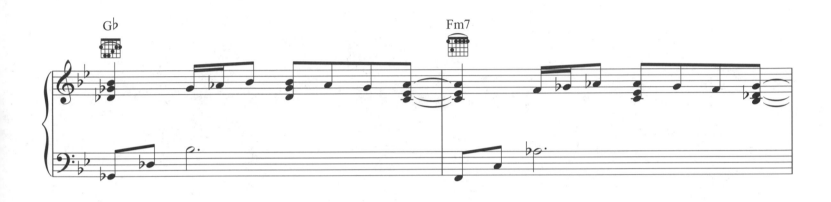

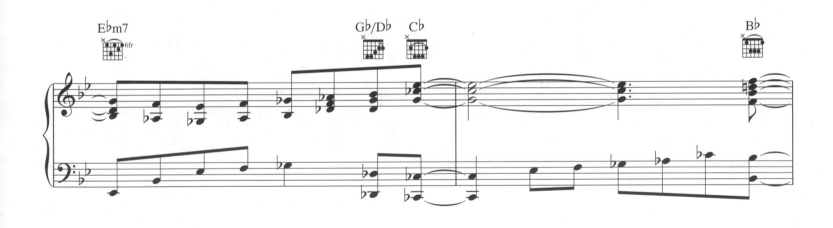

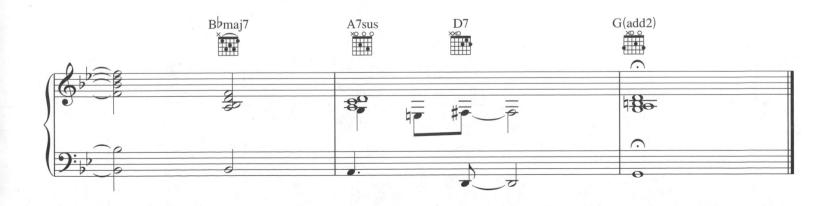

WELL ALRIGHT

Words and Music by CECE WINANS,
KEITH CROUCH and JOHN SMITH JR.

Times _ are hard- er now __ than __ they've ev- er been _

Cry- ing all __ night long, __ feel - ing like _ you're so __

WHAT ABOUT YOU

Words and Music by CECE WINANS
and TONY RICH

Ev - 'ry - bod - y's look - ing for a peace that flows,
Ev - 'ry - bod - y wants _ to ___ live life good.

More Contemporary Christian Folios from Hal Leonard

Arranged for Piano, Voice and Guitar

AMAZING GRACE
MUSIC INSPIRED BY THE MOTION PICTURE

Modern-day versions of 13 period hymns including: Amazing Grace (Chris Tomlin) • Fairest Lord Jesus (Natalie Grant) • Were You There? (Smokie Norful) • How Great Thou Art (Martina McBride) • more.
00313359 P/V/G...............$16.95

THE VERY BEST OF AVALON – TESTIFY TO LOVE

All 16 songs from the 2003 compilation by this acclaimed vocal quartet: Adonai • Can't Live a Day • Don't Save It All for Christmas Day • Everything to Me • Give It Up • Knockin' on Heaven's Door • New Day • Pray • Testify to Love • and more.
00306526 P/V/G...................$16.95

JEREMY CAMP – BEYOND MEASURE

This CD showcases Camp's powerful voice, which earned him back-to-back Male Vocalist of the Year GMA Dove Awards. Our songbook features all 12 tracks, including the hit single "What It Means" and: Beyond Measure • Everything • Give Me Jesus • Let It Fade • Tonight • more.
00306854 P/V/G.............................$16.95

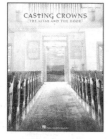

CASTING CROWNS – THE ALTAR AND THE DOOR

Matching folio to the album featuring 10 tracks: The Altar and the Door • East to West • Prayer for a Friend • Slow Fade • What This World Needs • The Word Is Alive • and more.
00306942 P/V/G...............$16.95

STEVEN CURTIS CHAPMAN – THIS MOMENT

Matching folio to Steven's 19th release featuring: Broken • Children of God • Cinderella • My Surrender • One Heartbeat • Something Crazy • With One Voice • You Are Being Loved • Yours.
00306941 P/V/G...............$16.95

AMY GRANT – GREATEST HITS

This collection has 19 of this popular singer's finest, including: Angels • Baby Baby • El Shaddai • Good for Me • I Will Remember You • Lead Me On • Simple Things • Takes a Little Time • and more.
00306948 P/V/G...............$17.95

DAVID CROWDER*BAND COLLECTION

David Crowder's innovative alt-pop style has made him one of today's most popular worship leaders. This collection includes 16 of his best songs: Here Is Our King • No One like You • Open Skies • Our Love Is Loud • You Alone • and more.
00306776 P/V/G.......................$16.95

STEVE GREEN – THE ULTIMATE COLLECTION

25 songs from the hits collection for this gospel star who got his start backing up Sandi Patti and the Gaither Vocal Band in the mid-'70s. Includes: Find Us Faithful • He Is Good • People Need the Lord • We Believe • What Wondrous Love Is This • and more.
00306784 P/V/G.......................$19.95

KUTLESS – STRONG TOWER

The 2005 release by this Christian hard rock band hailing from Oregon includes 13 tracks: We Fall Down • Take Me In • Ready for You • Draw Me Close • Better Is One Day • I Lift My Eyes Up • Word of God Speak • Arms of Love • and more.
00306726 P/V/G...................$16.95

MANDISA – TRUE BEAUTY

11 songs from the debut release by this former "American Idol" contestant. Songs include: God Speaking • He Will Come • Love Somebody • Oh, My Lord • Only the World • True Beauty • Unrestrained • Voice of a Savior.
00306934 P/V/G...............$16.95

NEWSBOYS – THE GREATEST HITS

18 songs from the popular alternative-CCM band, including: Entertaining Angels • I'm Not Ashamed • It Is You • Real Good Thing • Shine • Take Me to Your Leader • You Are My King (Amazing Love) • and more.
00306956 P/V/G...............$17.95

RECOLLECTION: THE BEST OF NICHOLE NORDEMAN

This collection features 17 releases from this popular CCM singer/songwriter, plus two new songs – "Sunrise" and "Finally Free." Includes: Brave • Holy • I Am • Is It Any Wonder? • River God • What If • Who You Are • Why • and more.
00306633 P/V/G.......................$17.95

SANCTUS REAL – WE NEED EACH OTHER

The fourth CD from this Dove Award-winning Toledo quintet features 10 songs: Black Coal • Eternal • Half Our Lives • Leap of Faith • Legacy • Sing • Turn On the Lights • We Need Each Other • and more.
00306976 P/V/G.......................$16.95

PHILLIPS, CRAIG & DEAN – THE ULTIMATE COLLECTION

31 of the greatest hits by this popular CCM trio. Includes: Crucified with Christ • Favorite Song of All • Here I Am to Worship • Lord, Let Your Glory Fall • Midnight Oil • Only You • Restoration • Shine on Us • This Is the Life • The Wonderful Cross • and more.
00306789 P/V/G.......................$19.95

MICHAEL W. SMITH – GREATEST HITS
2ND EDITION

25 of the best songs from this popular Contemporary Christian singer/songwriter, includes: Friends • I Will Be Here for You • Place in This World • Secret Ambition • This Is Your Time • You Are Holy (Prince of Peace) • and more.
00358186 P/V/G.......................$17.95

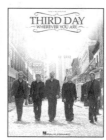

THIRD DAY – WHEREVER YOU ARE

This popular rock band's 2005 release features "Cry Out to Jesus" plus: Carry My Cross • Communion • Eagles • How Do You Know • I Can Feel It • Keep on Shinin' • Love Heals Your Heart • Mountain of God • Rise Up • The Sun Is Shining • Tunnel.
00306766 P/V/G.......................$16.95

THE CHRIS TOMLIN COLLECTION

15 songs from one of the leading artists and songwriters in contemporary Christian music, including the favorites: Amazing Grace (My Chains Are Gone) • Be Glorified • Holy Is the Lord • How Can I Keep from Singing • Take My Life • We Fall Down • and more.
00306951 P/V/G.......................$16.95

FOR MORE INFORMATION, SEE YOUR LOCAL MUSIC DEALER, OR WRITE TO:

7777 W. BLUEMOUND RD. P.O. BOX 13819 MILWAUKEE, WI 53213

For a complete listing of the products we have available, visit us online at www.halleonard.com

0408